Financial Freedom 3

How to Build, Plan & Invest in the Future

Build Now Plan to Invest For Your Future

By

Keith Outerbridge

Dedications:

I dedicate this book to my 2 Sons

Reese and **Ruben** Outerbridge

My Mom, **Camnine** Outerbridge

And my Outerbridge Family in both

Bermuda, California and New York City.

I Love You All and I hope this book will help you chart

YOUR Financial Freedom in the future.

Build, Plan & Invest in the Future!!!

Foreword

I decided to do a final installment to the Financial Freedom Series,
So I can incorporate all three books from experiences, knowledge and predicting future trends. As I said before, I was 100% percent correct in the predictions. I wanted to do something about it, so I wrote the 3rd & **final** installment Financial Freedom book series.

Economy turned bad, country at war, unemployment at an all-time high,
College graduates are unable to find jobs, debt crisis is in full swing,
People losing their homes and investments.

I pray and hope that this book will be a blueprint on **How to Build, Plan and Invest in the future?**

This is the third and FINAL installment of the series.
I did not write this book for financial gain, I only wish to help those individuals who want to reach Financial Freedom.

God Bless and May you seek Financial Freedom 3: Build, Plan & Invest.

Table of Content

Chapter 1- How Much Do You Think You Are Worth?

Chapter 2- How Much Income Do You Receive Daily?

Chapter 3- First You Build It.

Chapter 4 - The Planning Stage.

Chapter 5- Get Credit You Deserve.

Chapter 6 - Get a Second Income.

Chapter 7- Investing in the Future.

Introduction

Take a look at yourself and take a look at others. Look at those who are wealthy. Notice, that they all have a financial value put on themselves.

It is called "Net Worth. This is the value that is placed on individuals.

From celebrities to sports figures to actor/actresses, to any famous in this world, they all have a value placed on "How much they are worth?"

Ask this question of yourself?

How much are you worth in Today's Market?

Many people have gained and lost value in the market of success.

Net worth value is the total assets **minus** liabilities.

Go to http://www.celebritynetworth.com/ to learn & search who is your favorite celebrity and see what their net worth is calculated.

Write down on this notepad what you own and the value of it:

Chapter 1: How Much Do You Think Your Worth?

In today's job market you are valued as either an asset to the company or a liability. When you become a liability for a company that is when you get fired or laid-off. A Liability is an expense to the company. They find you expendable and overall an expensive employee to have in the corporation. To be an asset to a company one must be able to work full time or part-time and be able to do overtime.

But as the years going forward show, companies are reversing that trend. As shown in chart below:

According to the Department of Labor, companies are now seeking to hire more part-time workers than full-time, in order to cut cost and expenses. Currently, all workers are now starting to be a liability if they work over 40 hours. The bottom line is to do more with less workers and the profits will show. Companies are now realizing that they can do more and make more money with less, by cutting worker's salaries and moving them into part-time positions. Full time positions will soon the thing of the past. **Part-timers** will likely get to **keep their jobs** without benefits, so that the company will prosper in the long run.

Let's take a look at what you are **worth** to a company.

Calculate your **years of experience** in the field of interest (+) *Plus*

Educational Degrees, Certifications and ability to learn. *Equals* (=) What you are <u>**worth to a company?**</u> The value is determined by your credentials in the job market, in order to compete with existing individuals who are similar to your background in a working environment.

Based on **who you are and what abilities you have**, will determine what a company is willing to pay for you. You can be **paid** by the *hour, weekly, bi-weekly or monthly salary.* This simple calculation has tried to match individuals with companies who are searching for new hire employees. In order to get these positions, one must possess skills in education, experience and ability to <u>**"Think outside the Box".**</u> Meaning *be creative* to *new ideas and learning.* If you have these skills, then working for a company who wants new innovative ideas will be for you.

For Example; a company like Google hires only the smartest individuals who can *think for themselves* without anyone telling them how to think. They are the most *creative individuals* who want to create **something new**. This is a new trend for hiring people and becoming a successful employee. Both as an individual and company as a whole, the creative employees are the new talent in their company.

To become a part of this trend,
"THINK FOR YOURSELF and BE VERY CREATIVE IN YOUR THINKING."

Fortune 500 companies are looking for individuals who will think for themselves with limited supervision. Ideas are needed to stay innovative and profitable.

The Value of an employee holds true to a company, when they see the willingness to create and Think for the benefit of the company.

Many companies have adopted this model of success with employees by giving them the opportunity to show case their mental skills.

Once they are employed by the company, they are expecting them to build, create and think about company interest only.

They have now become a highly valued employee to assist them in difficult financial times, in order to achieve the highest goal possible within the company agenda. These employees will be the most valuable in the company and will have all the perks of ownership in the company without ever being owners themselves.

As an employee looks forward to retirement age, companies will devalue their employee's net worth in a company.

Read below a study taken in Canada 2006 about the new hire in the 21ˢᵗ Century workplace.

Taken from the website: http://www.iveybusinessjournal.com/topics/the-workplace/a-newemployment-deal-for-the-21st-century-workplace#.UgVGL_PD9ol

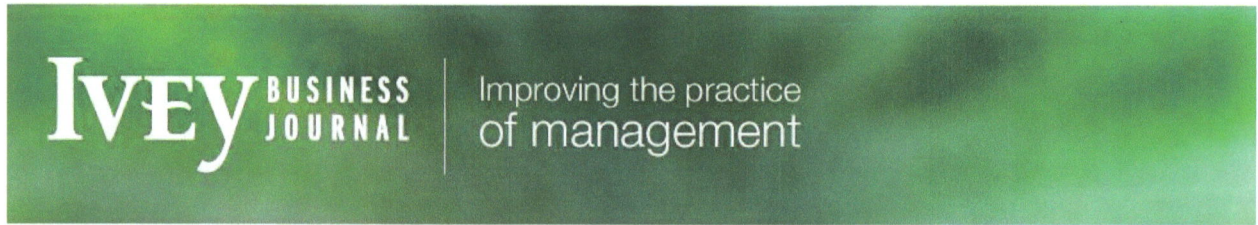

A NEW EMPLOYMENT DEAL FOR THE 21ST CENTURY WORKPLACE

by Kevin Asselstine and Keri Alletson
The Workplace | March / April 2006

Share on emailEmailShare on twitterShare on TwitterShare on facebookPost to FacebookShare on linkedinShare on LinkedInShare on deliciousSave to DeliciousShare on instapaperSave to InstapaperPrint

As these authors write, a new paradigm is settling in and occupying top managers' waking hours. It's one that focuses on workforce effectiveness, managing talent, and reinventing the core employment value proposition. The companies that will win in this era are those that deploy people in new ways to accomplish their business objectives and deliver both personal and organizational growth.

The start of the century has seen a number of discrete changes in the workforce-workplace arena, varying in size and impact. Considered individually, these change present nothing more than another bump in the road for organizations. Considered collectively, they add up to a red flag for all employers, in Canada and around the world. This article will examine these red flags, share new research on the views of employees, and propose a "new deal" for workforce management.

THE NEW WORKPLACE

Many mature organizations are experiencing sharp increases in operating costs, driven by legacy issues and workforce programs such as pensions, benefits, and salaries. At the same time, small and large employers alike are under pressure from shareholders to accelerate growth. At the same time, the strategies they are using – such as improving customer intimacy and innovation – are more people-intensive than ever before. The result is increased pressure to retain talent, to build succession plans for current leaders, and to develop new ways of "incenting" employees to achieve business growth objectives. Across the board, organizations around the world are experiencing challenges in maintaining the right mix of people, with the right skills, available at the right time.

Above all, there appears to be something of a crisis in employee motivation and "engagement" at work. As the new Towers Perrin Global Workforce study[1] shows, less than one in 5 Canadians are highly engaged by their work. Globally, only 14 percent of employees are highly engaged. Many more (62 percent globally and 66 percent in Canada) are only moderately engaged, creating a substantial retention risk and also affecting the organization's ability to excel. Moderately engaged workers are not only significantly more likely to leave the organization

(see Exhibit 1), but are also considerably less likely to contribute to the achievement of broad company objectives. This issue is often characterized as poor morale, but it more likely stems from an organization's failure to create an engaged workforce that encourages employees to exert the discretionary effort required to help their company truly succeed (see side-bar). This is a somewhat complex topic, but the issue boils down to a fundamental lack of alignment between what the employer and the employee expect of one another. This can be thought of in a number of different ways – the "employer promise", the "performance contract", or the "employment value proposition.". For the sake of simplicity in this article, we refer to this mutual commitment as "the deal".

Exhibit 1:
Highly engaged employees are more likely to stay

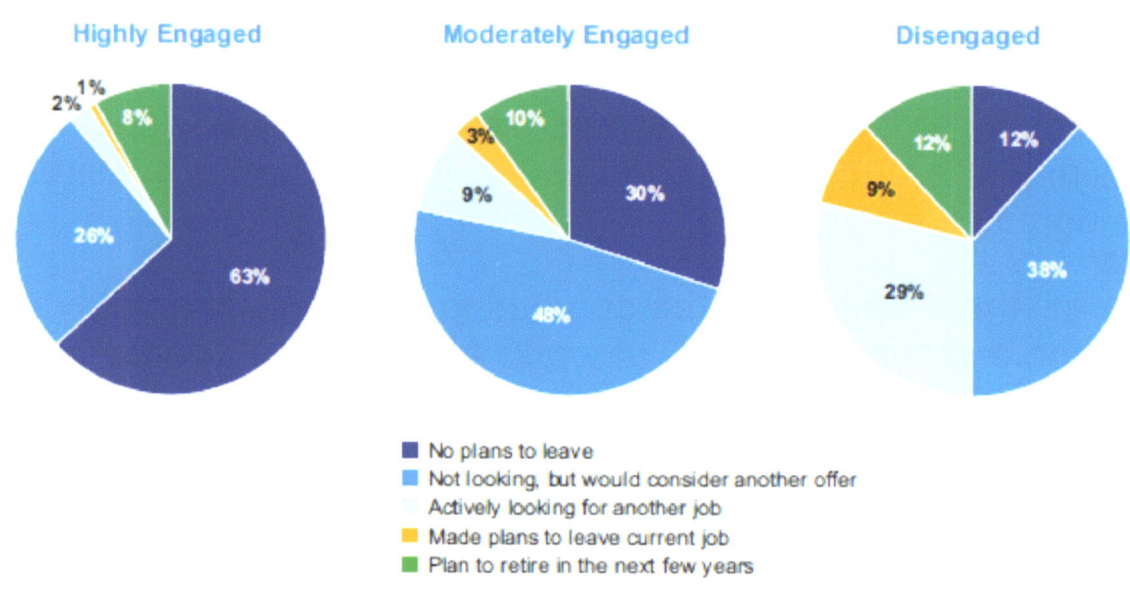

Source: *Towers Perrin Global Workforce Study — Canada*

A simple illustration of this approach can be seen in Exhibit 2. We use this model to examine both the employer and employee needs from the "deal" perspective, factoring in external elements that will also influence the strategy. The organization's "human capital" strategy basically looks at how to staff the business plan. The organization's "total rewards" strategy, derived from that strategy, defines the value proposition for employees in joining an organization, and making a contribution.

Exhibit 2:
Total rewards strategy should reinforce the human capital strategy

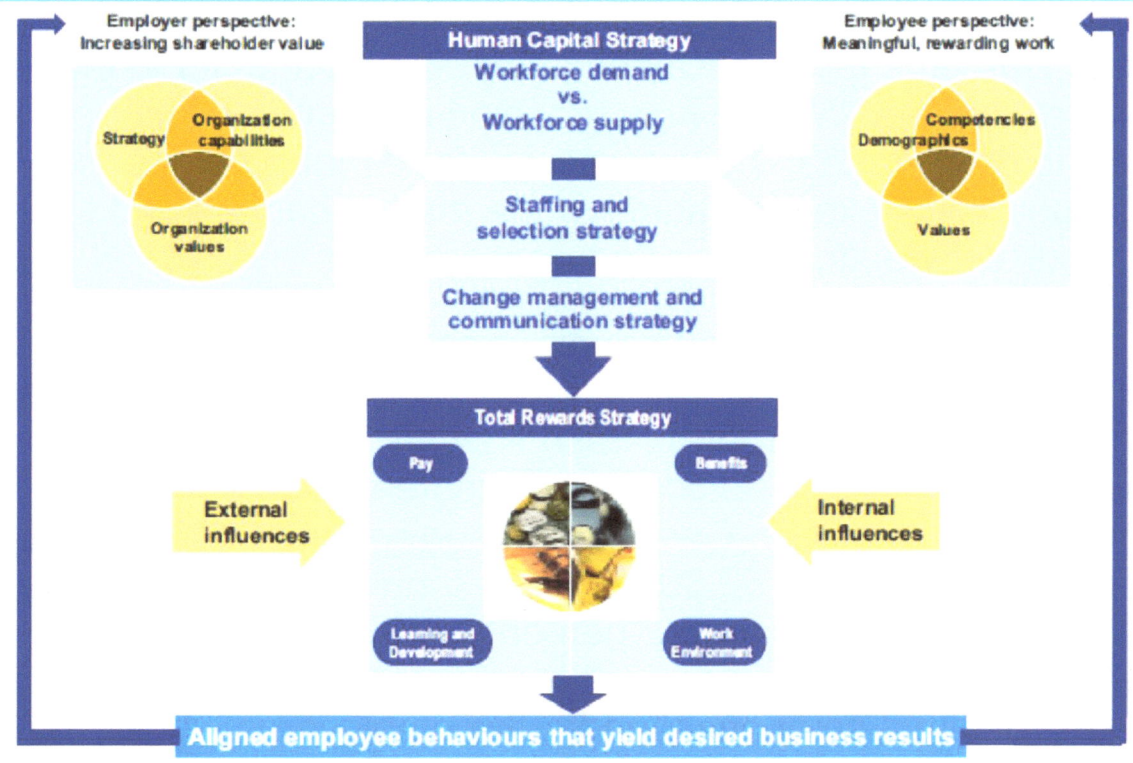

© Towers Perrin

WHAT DOES THE "OLD DEAL" LOOK LIKE?

For much of the last century, the "deal" was fairly clear. In exchange for their labor, employees could expect a high degree of job security and a slow but steady increase in their expected total compensation. Learning and development were provided, as long as they were specific to the job. Career-long loyalty was rewarded with financial support in retirement years (in the form of pension income and/or retiree medical subsidies). Organization structure meant that with annual increases and the gradual accumulation of relevant experience, the best people could climb the ladder within their units, and set their sights on a management role. In part because there was essentially just one career ladder/path available within a department, organizational titles proliferated.

Over the past decade or so, this deal has been under significant pressure as organizations have flattened, cut costs, used technology to increase productivity output expectations from existing staff, and faced escalating competition both for workers and for customers. We are now reaching a point where constant tweaks to the "old deal" no longer work for either employers or employees. Let's examine some of the major changes and stresses on the current workforce management system.

Red flag: Rising labor costs Corporate pension plans designed in the mid-twentieth century are increasing in both absolute cost and volatility, influencing corporate cash flow and long-term financial viability. Health care costs continue to increase in double digit increments each year (in Canada, the current annual average per-employee cost is about $2,500[2]). While individual salaries have increased only by three to four percent each year for the last several years, this figure does not reflect "real" salary inflation. The total cost of direct compensation for the employer is higher, in part because many organizations are making contributions to their retirement fund and health benefits.

---

[1] The Towers Perrin Global Workforce study examines current attitudes about work with over 85,000 full-time employees in 16 countries, on 4 continents.

[2] Source: Towers Perrin Health Care Cost Study, Canada 2005-2006.

This study was done in Canada 2006 and it holds true today in America as well. Notice how many workers become disengaged in working as they reach retirement age in exhibit 1.

The New Value of Employees for the Future Workforce

The value of workers in the future will be more diverse in the workplace and community. Due to high technological advancements in the industry, computers, laptops, tablets and smartphones will cater to a new employee, who will have to be highly skilled. College education will help, but the trend will be so advanced that colleges will not be able to keep up with the demand of new technology. Thus, understanding your value of worth to a company, will be determined by your absolute knowledge of technological advancements in any and all industries.

Value and worth will be placed on every worker to see if you have the ability to comprehend and learn quickly the technology. As time moves forward, companies will only value the highly skilled and competent individuals in their job and will only keep those who can make a contribution to their industry. All other workers who are not skilled will be let go, fired or laid-off.

Now that you know how companies value their employees.

Let's examine your net worth value to YOURSELF.

Remember the notepad listing of writing down what you own and the value of it. This is your net value asset. For Example; if you own a house that cost $300,000, but the market value is $400,000, this is your net total asset value to YOU. If you own a car and it is worth $5,000 on the buyer's market. This is your asset value of ownership and will be added to your net worth. When calculated, this will be your net value worth to YOURSELF. **Ownership is the key to your net worth.** This is held as value to how much you are worth. By owning property, material wealth and objects of value such as gold, jewelry etc. It all gets calculated as value to YOU. The Total Ownership of Asset values you own minus (-) your liabilities and expenses, **"What you owe"**, Is your net worth.

To increase your net worth is to own more things of value so that you can quickly sell to make a profit. Determine how much you are worth by adding up all of your total ownership of merchandises, such as Houses, Car, jewelry, Investments etc.

Then you will get a good idea about how much you are worth in the market.

Chapter 2: How Much Income Do You Receive Daily?

If there was a job listing that read this sign, many people would apply for it. Getting paid on a daily basis is a great thing. To receive money every day, is a dream come true.

Question: So why do companies pay you weekly, bi-weekly or monthly and make you wait for your paycheck?

Answer: They want to see you perform first, then see if you can make them enough money so they don't have to pay you until later.

The Bottom Line: *"Make the Company Money First, then we will talk about compensating you later".*

As they say **"a day's work is a day's pay."**

But most companies will never pay you like that. So in terms of your value as an employee to them, Money will determine your value in the company and in how much you make for them.

Companies put high stringent on employees to be educated, globally diverse thinking, creative etc. All of which is needed to make money for them not you.

Now let's look at how much money you bring in for yourself.

If you work and receive an income, then you are able to receive monies on a regular basis. However, you also have to account for your expenses and bills daily and whatever is left over is yours.

This is your real income you bring home.

A Study was done on Sources of Income in New Zealand in 2006.

What Happened to People's Sources of income?

Wage and salary income was the primary source of income in 2006, with 54.9 percent of people, receiving income from this source. Investment income was received by 32.4 percent of people, government transfers by 29.5 percent, self-employed by 11.4 percent, other transfers by 1.8 percent, and no source of income by 9.2 percent. The introduction of the Working for Families package has seen an increase in the number of people who are eligible for government subsidies, and this is reflected in an increase in the proportion of people receiving government income (up from 27.3 percent in the June 2006 quarter). It is possible for a person to receive more than one source of income.

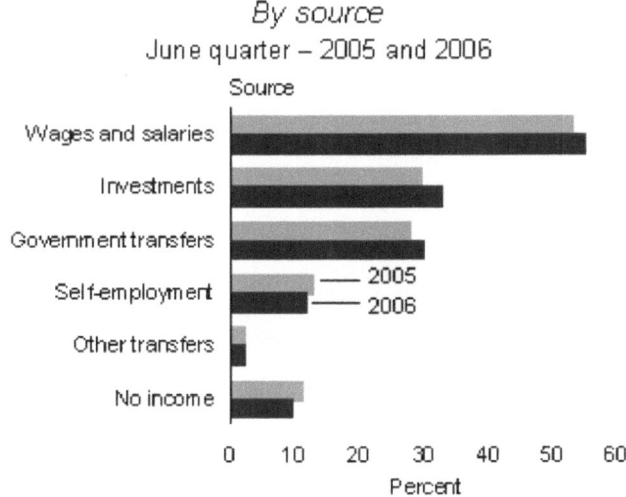

Wage and salary income

Average weekly income from wages and salaries for those in paid employment increased from $592 in the June 2005 quarter to $619 (4.7 percent) in the June 2006 quarter. People in paid employment are defined as those who receive income from wages and salaries and/or selfemployment.

Average weekly wage and salary income for people receiving income from wages and salaries was $739 in the June 2006 quarter, an increase of $21 (2.9 percent) on the June 2005 quarter. This is consistent with an increase of 3.6 percent in average weekly earnings over the same period, as measured by the Quarterly Employment Survey for the June 2006 quarter.

Average hourly earnings for people receiving income from wages and salaries in the June 2006 quarter were $20.04, an increase of $0.74 (3.9 percent) from the same period last year. This was mainly due to an increase for females of $1.19 (6.9 percent), whereas hourly earnings for males increased by $0.29 (1.4 percent).

Median hourly earnings also rose (up $0.90 to $17.00) with increases of $0.63 for males (to $18.13) and $0.88 for females (to $15.88). Comparing female earnings with male earnings, the ratio of median hourly earnings was 87.6 percent in the June 2006 quarter. Over the last 10 years (the life of the survey), the ratio between male and female median hourly earnings has improved, from 83.0 percent in the June 1997 quarter to 87.6 percent in the June 2006 quarter.

Industries with significant increases in average hourly earnings for people receiving income from wages and salaries were education (4.0 percent), wholesale and retail trade (5.3 percent), and other services (5.6 percent).

Significant increases in average hourly earnings for people receiving income from wages and salaries occurred in the following occupations: service and sales workers (6.1 percent) and elementary occupations (5.3 percent).

Distribution of average weekly income from all sources

Income quintiles divide the population into five groups by ranking people in order by the amount of income they receive. The bottom quintile (quintile 1) is the lowest 20 percent of the population, in terms of income, while the top quintile (quintile 5) is the highest 20 percent of the population. In the June 2006 quarter, the top quintile comprised those with weekly incomes of $920 and over, while those in the bottom quintile received weekly incomes of under $190.

In the June 2006 quarter, 11.3 percent of females were in the top quintile and 23.8 percent were in the bottom quintile. In contrast, 29.1 percent of males were in the top quintile and 15.8 percent were in the bottom quintile.

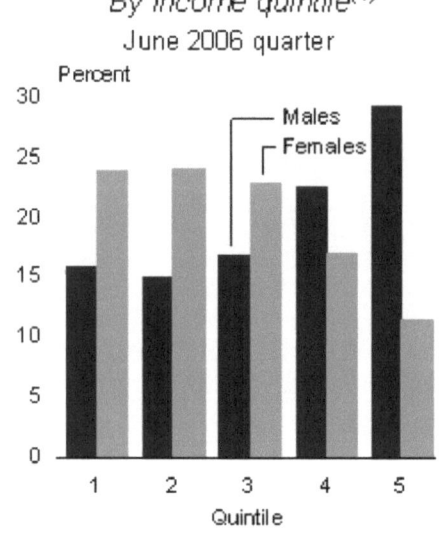

(1) All sources of income.

Dispersion of employment income

Typically, income from self-employment is more dispersed than income from wages and salaries. The June 2006 quarter figures continued to reflect this. The quintile ranges for those receiving income from selfemployment and wages and salaries for the June 2006 quarter are shown in the table below. The bottom quintile includes those who receive a loss from self-employment income.

	Weekly income	
	Self-employment	Wages and salaries
Quintile 1	under $192	under $354
Quintile 2	$192 to $498	$354 to $575
Quintile 3	$499 to $766	$576 to $759
Quintile 4	$767 to $1,150	$760 to $1,035
Quintile 5	$1,151 and over	$1,036 and over

Investment income

The average weekly income from investments for all people was $33 in the June 2006 quarter, compared with $31 in the same period last year. Income from investments was received by 32.4 percent of all people in the June 2006 quarter, compared with 29.2 percent in the June 2005 quarter.

Investment income varies with age. The 60- to 64-year age group received the highest average weekly investment income of $88, whereas the 65 years and over age group received average weekly investment income of $66. All age groups under 30 years received an average investment income of $6 or less.

The average weekly investment income for those receiving investment income was $106. The age groups receiving the highest average weekly investment income for those receiving investment income were the 55- to 59-year and the 60- to 64-year age groups ($144 and $191, respectively).

All age groups under 30 years received an average investment income of $31 or less.

Self-employed earners

In the June 2006 quarter, the proportion of people receiving self-employment income was 11.4 percent, down from 12.5 percent in the June 2005 quarter. This group received an average weekly self-employment income of $821, up from $815 for the same period last year.

The 45- to 49-year and the 55- to 59-year age groups had the highest proportion of people earning a component of their total income from self-employment in the June 2006 quarter (20.0 and 20.8 percent, respectively).

Government transfers

Government transfers include income from benefits, family support, student allowances, Accident Compensation Corporation, New Zealand Superannuation, and veterans and war pensions. The introduction of the Working for Families package has seen an increase in the number of people who are eligible for government transfers, and this is reflected in an increase in the proportion of people receiving government transfer income.

The percentage of people aged 15 years and over receiving income from government transfers in the June 2006 quarter was 29.5 percent, compared with 27.3 percent in the June 2005 quarter. A higher proportion of females (35.3 percent) received government transfer income than males (23.5 percent). Both of these proportions were higher than those recorded in the June 2005 quarter, which were 32.3 percent for females and 22.0 percent for males.

For those receiving income from government transfers, average weekly income from this source in the June 2006 quarter was $244, compared with $247 in the June 2005 quarter. The median income from government transfers for this group rose from $235 in the June 2005 quarter to $239 in the June 2006 quarter.

Ethnic group statistics

Average weekly income from all sources in the June 2006 quarter was $658 for European/Pākehā, $506 for Māori, $434 for Pacific peoples and $460 for the 'Other' ethnic group.

The following table compares the distribution of income by age group for Māori and the total population.

Age group	Average weekly income from paid employment for those in paid employment		Average weekly income for all people from all sources	
	Māori	Total population	Māori	Total population
15-24	$465	$442	$251	$287
25-34	$667	$771	$563	$667
35-44	$728	$883	$649	$797
45-54	$756	$863	$732	$814
55-64	$662	$789	$536	$681

The different age structures of the ethnic groups have an impact on income comparisons. The Māori, Pacific peoples and 'Other' ethnic groups have proportionally more people in the younger age groups, particularly the 15- to 24-year age group, who have lower average earnings. The majority of those aged 65 years and over are in the European/Pākehā ethnic group, for whom the major source of income is New Zealand Superannuation.

Age group statistics

In the June 2006 quarter, the highest average weekly income for all people from all sources was received by the 45- to 49-year age group ($827). Looking at each sex, for males, the 35- to 39-year age group received the highest weekly income from all sources ($1,065), and for females it was the 50- to 54-year age group ($624).

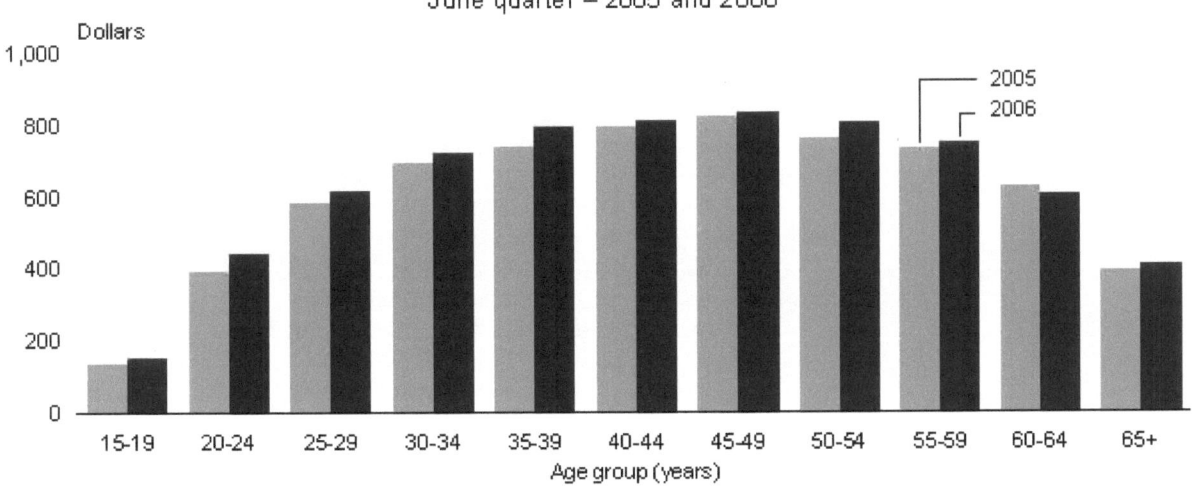

For people in paid employment, the 35- to 39-year age group received the highest average weekly income ($939), followed by the 45- to 49-year age group ($933) and the 40- to 44-year age group ($919). The lowest average weekly incomes for those in paid employment were received by the 15- to 19-year age group ($289) and the 20- to 24-year age group ($576). The highest average weekly income for those not in paid employment was $343, which was for people aged 65 years and over.

For full-time wage and salary earners, the 35- to 39-year age group had the highest average weekly wage and salary income ($1,003), and this age group received average weekly part-time wage and salary income of $369. For part-time wage and salary earners, the highest average weekly wage and salary income was received by the 30- to 34-year age group ($386).

Regional statistics

Average weekly income from all sources for all people in the June 2006 quarter was highest in Auckland ($625), Wellington ($672) and Canterbury ($642). The lowest was for Manawatu-Wanganui ($521).

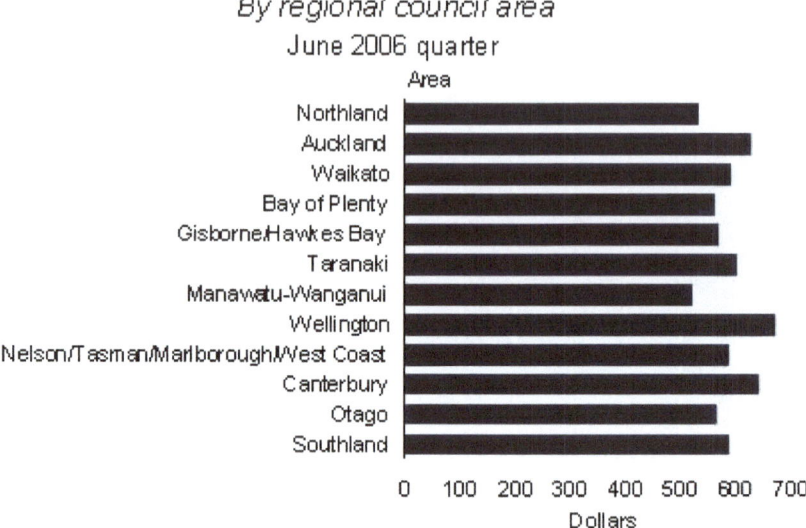

Household statistics

The average weekly household income from all sources was $1,321 in the June 2006 quarter, an increase of 4.8 percent from the June 2005 quarter average of $1,260. Median weekly household income from all sources rose 8.6 percent (to $1,129). 'One parent with dependent children only' households received the lowest average weekly household income of $574, up from $537 in the June 2005 quarter, while 'Couple with adult child(ren) only and other(s)' received the highest average weekly income of $2,103, up from $2,031 in the June 2005 quarter.

For technical information contact:
Janelle Foster or Adele Dunleavy

Wellington 04 931 4600   04 931 4600**mail:** info@stats.govt.nz

This study was taken from New Zealand Department of Statistics in 2006. It still holds true today, Sources of income through Wages and Salary, Investments, Government Social Programs. Other countries have similar programs to U.S and sounds very familiar to us. Investments, Self-Employment, and Household income are derived from Sources of Income for ethnic groups, ages and regional stats.

These statistics show the correlation between age, group, and race in regards to Household income. Although, the study was done in 2006 in New Zealand, the same problems also applies to The United States.

Sources of income are from wages and salary. Investment income and government subsidies and programs, also count towards income.

Based on Age, Race and Region, all people will have to understand their value and net worth to themselves. As you get older your income drops and becomes a fixed asset.

In every country, the source of income is valuable to individuals in order to see if they can side with the cost of living in their region.

Underdeveloped countries rely on sources of income to be above the poverty line. When you are not meeting the goals of your living needs, then you will fall into poverty. Not being able to keep up with the cost of living is very important in any country and society because it is part of your basic need to live.

Although these studies were done in 2006, in today's environment it holds true about the value of your daily income and sources of income in your country. Receiving income on a daily basis is key to understanding wealth for long and short term financial goals.

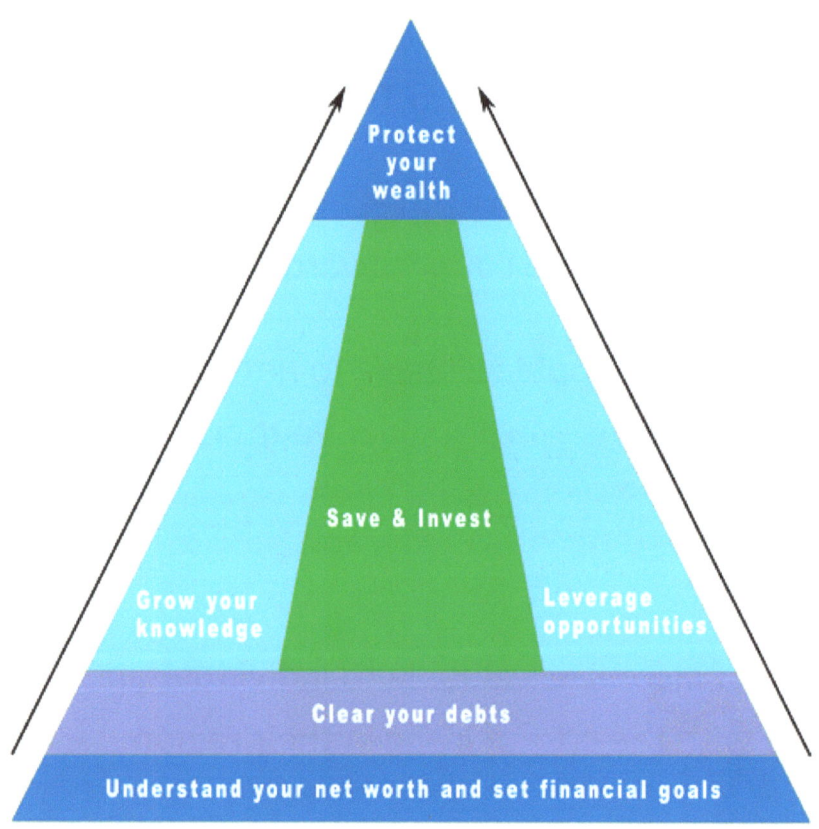

First, clear your debts, **Second**, determine your income daily, **Third**, Save & Invest, **Fourth**, protect your wealth as seen in above diagram.

Chapter 3: First You Build It

In order for you to seek wealth, you must begin with what you have. Let's Build Wealth from the beginning.

First go to my book….. Financial Freedom One: A Special Guide to Understanding Investing…

Read Chapter: How to get a Dollar on **page 28.**

Successful Guide to Starting Your Own Business. Once you understand this chapter you can then move on to *Financial Freedom Too:* **Surviving the Lay-Off Era, Read Pages 22, 23, 55.** Then go to Financial Freedom One: A Special Guide to Understanding Investing, **Read pages 30 to 32**. These chapters show you how to get a dollar, save the dollar and invest in an asset management account earning interest on your dollar. For Example; personally, after every night when I come home from a hard day at work, I take all the loose change in my pocket and put it in a jar. Quarters, Nickels, Dimes and Pennies all add up at the end of the day. On average I save about $30.00 dollars a month in coins saved. It may not sound like a lot, but remember this is monies that I had in my pocket. ***Spare change for the day and week*** added for the month. The goal of building wealth first is **Savings.**

You must be able to save on a daily basis, which would turn to weekly and monthly. Put away **10% of your wages** to **yourself.** *Be consistent* and do it every day. You will determine your wealth on what you bring home every day. Every penny counts and will eventually add up over the days, weeks, and month. This is the beginning of Building It First Wealth. Once you have a daily count of income

Receiving daily, then you can Read my book <u>Financial Freedom One</u>: A Special Guide to Understanding Investing. **Read pages 85 to 87**

Keep in mind that both books are needed to assist you with building your wealth as well. If you have not purchased the 2 books, you need to use them as references. The books are available online and they are:

Financial Freedom One: A Special Guide to Understanding Investing

https://www.createspace.com/3739260

Financial Freedom Too: Surviving the Lay-Off Era

https://www.createspace.com/3739248

Both books can be purchased online at Amazon.com or Barnes & Noble

Chapter 4: The Planning Stage

Learn to Invest at 24 to 34 years old

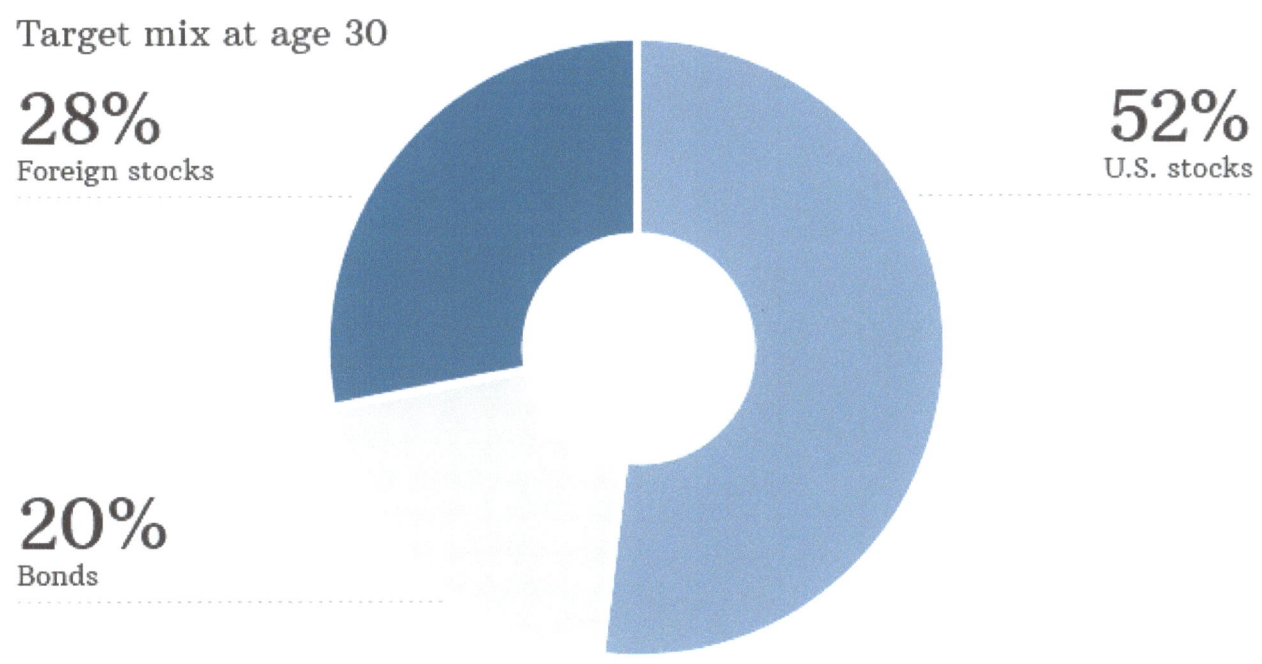

During this time of your life between 24 & 34 of age, invest aggressively in U.S. Stocks to get a higher return.

Read **Financial Freedom One: A Special Guide to Investing**,

Pages 10 to 23. Learn about the different types of investments, safe haven investments and how stocks operate on the World market.

Investing at a young age will build wealth for the future.

Learn to Invest at 35 to 45

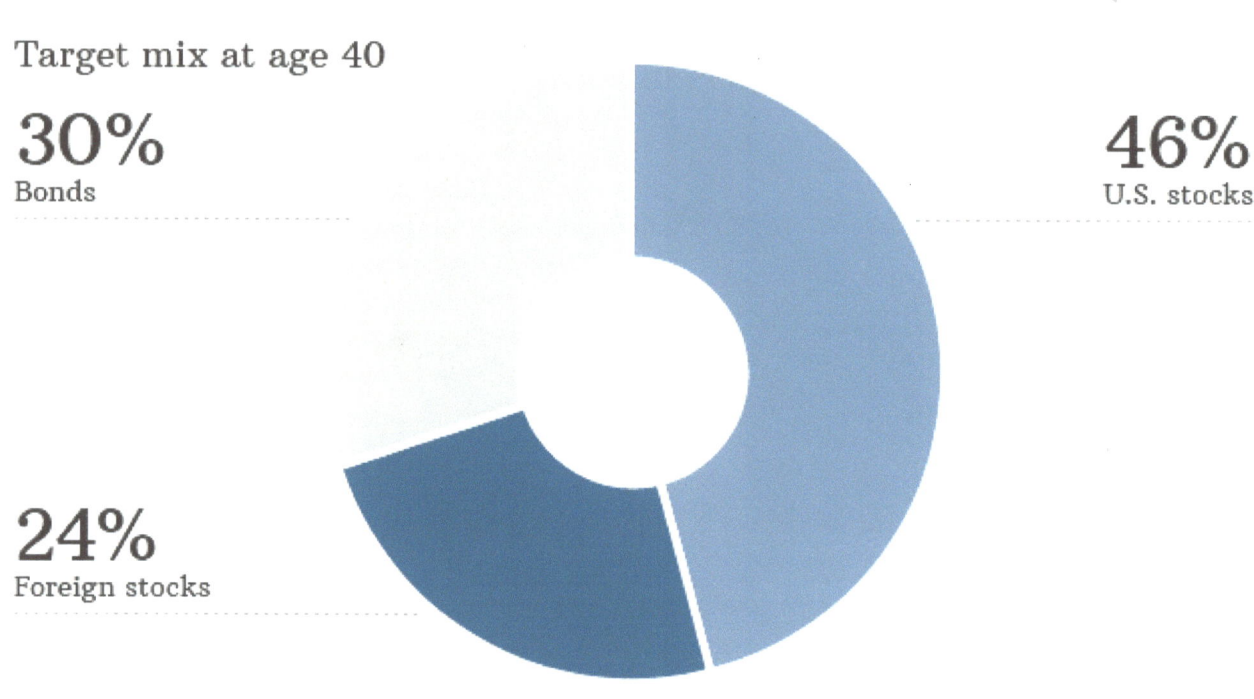

Target mix at age 40

30% Bonds

46% U.S. stocks

24% Foreign stocks

NOTES: SAVINGS GOALS CALCULATIONS ASSUME RETIREMENT AT AGE 65; 80% PRE-RETIREMENT INCOME REPLACEMENT RATE; SOCIAL SECURITY BENEFIT; 5% INITIAL WITHDRAWAL RATE. SOURCES: INDEX FUNDS ADVISORS/IFA.COM (MODEL PORTFOLIOS); CHARLES FARRELL, NORTHSTAR INVESTMENT ADVISORS (SAVINGS TARGETS)

During this time of your life, introduce yourself to Bonds & Mutual Funds. Read **Financial Freedom One: A Special Guide to Investing**,

Pages 13 to 15. Learn about Bonds and how they work & Mutual Funds Listed to help chart your path to financial freedom.

Investing during this stage of your life, is the median of understanding and learning about various types of investments. Read these pages to learn more about the risk and safety of these investments during times as you approach retirement.

Learn to Invest 46 to 54

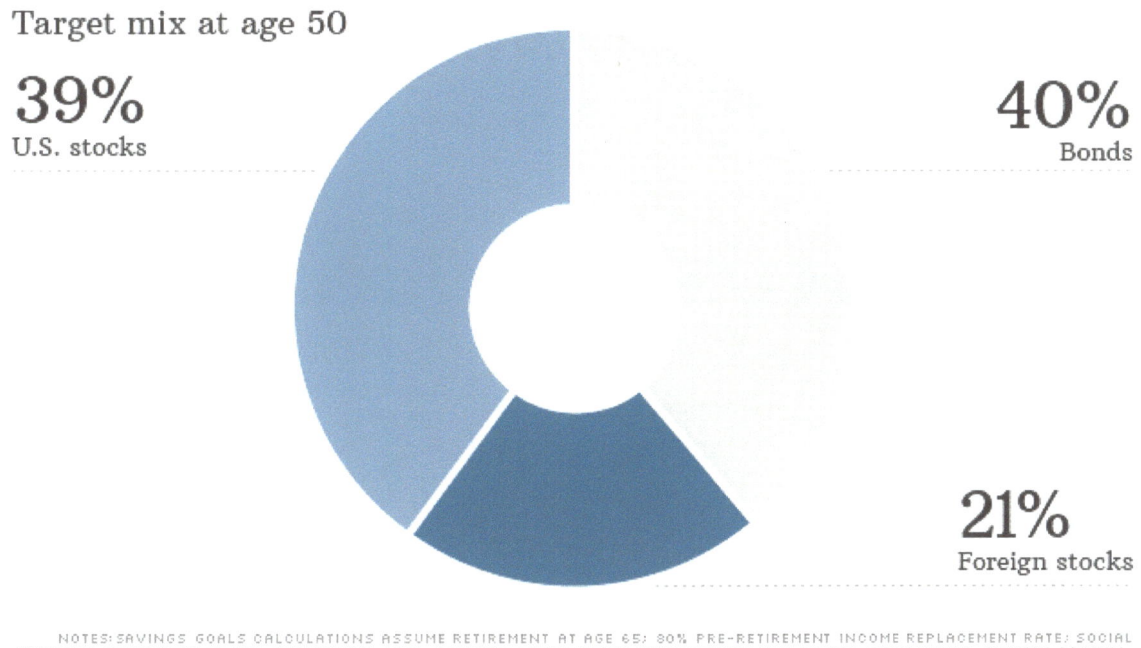

Target mix at age 50

39% U.S. stocks

40% Bonds

21% Foreign stocks

NOTES: SAVINGS GOALS CALCULATIONS ASSUME RETIREMENT AT AGE 65; 80% PRE-RETIREMENT INCOME REPLACEMENT RATE; SOCIAL SECURITY BENEFIT; 5% INITIAL WITHDRAWAL RATE. SOURCES: INDEX FUNDS ADVISORS/IFA.COM (MODEL PORTFOLIOS); CHARLES FARRELL, NORTHSTAR INVESTMENT ADVISORS (SAVINGS TARGETS)

As you reach your Golden Years, **Savings** now become **Investments** to live off your **interest bearing accounts, Social Security, Pension Funds** and *hopefully a business that you can allow your kids or grandkids to run for you*. Read **Financial Freedom Too: Surviving the Lay-Off Era**,

Pages 42 to 46. Learn about Market Timing, Seasonal Investing and choosing an investment that's safe. Investing more in Bonds and Safe investments and not risky investments in needed to survive during times of retirement. This book will help you understand when the country is in a Recession and you are not in a position to be hired due to your older age, you can survive during rough times.

Keep in mind that you want investments to have a safe rate of return so you can be able to live off the interest of them.

Planning during your youthful years would be helpful, but if you are in a position of not accumulating wealth earlier on in life, then you must consider starting or owning a business at this time. It will still put you ahead of the game of retirement and allow you to build and plan your retirement in the coming years.

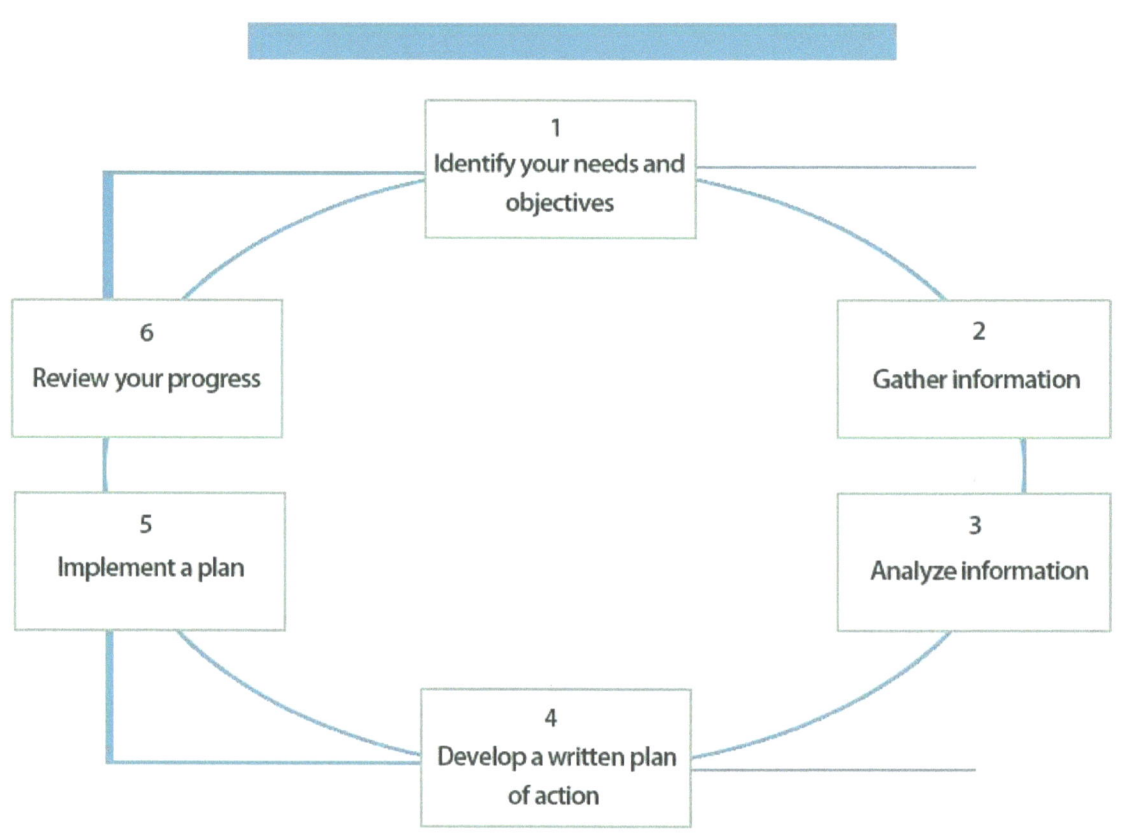

First, Identify <u>What You Need?</u>

Are you in need of a ***<u>job</u>***, ***<u>money</u>***, ***<u>Item</u>*** you wish to ***<u>purchase</u>***?

Then read **Financial Freedom Too: Surviving the Lay-Off Era**,

Pages 10 to 15, a List is provided on Recession Proof Jobs that are hiring right now. Use this list and what they pay to plan to get the job you need that is popular during difficult economic times. Gather all the information that is needed, schooling and certifications to pursue these jobs. Your plan should consist of building and writing a resume to cater to these jobs descriptions and go get the necessary education to get these jobs. Then follow up consistently with phone calls, emails and letters to the company.

If it is money you need then read **Financial Freedom One: A Special Guide to Understanding Investing**, **Pages 27 to 30**. How to get a dollar. How to Start a Business of your own and get money for it.

There are businesses out there that you can start with little or no up cost money to start. These businesses will allow you to be creative and there is no limit to the amount of money you can make. In this book is a list of businesses you can start right away. Read each business and see if it is for you.

If you wish to invest in a Business, read **Financial Freedom Too: Surviving the Lay-Off Era**, **Pages 22 to 36.** A List is provided for you to choose and read about various recession proof businesses and how to start them right away. The information is provided for you with telephone numbers and websites for your access. Please use them and start your business now.

If you plan to purchase a large ticket item, save and invest combination is needed until you reach your goal. Investing and saving is a great combination to building and planning for what you need in the future.

Review your progress and measure what you need to do to get closer to your goal. Your plan of action depends on you and how determined you are to reach your goal. Please put a realistic Plan in place to accomplish your goal. Start small and build. Use common sense and realistic measures to accomplish what you need.

Whatever you wish to accomplish, Build it and Plan accordingly.

Make sure you set real goals to get to where you need to be in life.

You're Work Sheet of Life

I Need to Buy...	What is the Time Frame?	Begin Date	What you did?	Who did You Phone Called?	End Date	Did You Reach Your Goal?

Set up a chart like this in order to find what it is you want, how you plan to accomplish it and how long it will take to achieve your goal.

Mention what you did to achieve this goal. Who did you phone call or contact to get you closer to your goal? Then finally, mark down when you started and ended the date to reach your goal.

This is just an idea or chart to help you get started in navigating to your goal. Use this chart as a sample to writing down and measuring the progress of what you did to get closer to your goal.

In determining your goal, first you need to get rid of debt

Say Goodbye to Debt

Over extended credit cards. Braces for the kids. Reduced hours at work. Unexpected car repairs. Most of us will face some or all of these scenarios, at some point in time. If you're in this situation now, you may be wondering how you'll ever save more money, especially if you have mounting debt. However, even when it seems impossible, there are steps you can take to pay down debt. And when you do, you can save more, and continue building your wealth. Consider these possibilities:

Debt

Home Planning

Finding a Solution

Use the Calculators

Seek a Financial Advisor

Learn More About Cash Flow

Examine Your Cash Flow

Sometimes, you can uncover ways to save just by keeping track of expenses for a month. When you're running with day-to-day activities, it can be difficult to notice how much you are spending on coffees, lunches, or magazines grabbed at the drug store. However, when you see these purchases totaled on paper, it gives you a different perspective. This often makes it easier to change the way you do things, to cut expenses, and find extra money.

Consolidate High Interest Debts

Unsecured, high-interest debts such as credit cards, department store cards, loans, or lines of credit can cost you hundreds – even thousands – of dollars in interest every year. If you have several debts like this, or if the balance on your credit card is a little too high, a consolidation loan can help. Folding your debts into one, lower interest loan will save you money. You can then use these savings to pay off your debts faster.

Save On Your Mortgage

When did you get your mortgage? For many of us, it was before interest rates dropped. This means you may be able to refinance your mortgage, which could reduce your payments by hundreds of dollars every month. For example, reducing the interest you pay from 5% to 3% on a $100,000 mortgage could save you approximately $200 every month. You can use these savings to pay down high interest debts.

Even Small Changes Can Save You Hundreds of Dollars Every Year on your Mortgage.

<small>At Lifesource Financial Management, we will work together to help you reduce your expenses and find new ways to save. We will guide you through a monthly budget and help uncover new savings. We will present different solutions and options. We will walk through the pros and cons of the solutions and together determine the best options for you and your family.</small>

By planning and getting rid of your debts or keeping them under controlled, certain expenses will keep you at bay. Mortgage, rent utility bills are all a given to pay in expenses. However, having multiple incomes coming in will have organize and pay for these expenses.

Chapter 5- Get the Credit You Deserve

Credit beginners usually have but one question,

"How do I get credit"? All the details about getting credit will follow, but the simple answer is, "Apply for it."

Where to Apply For Credit

The best way for a beginner to get credit is to apply for a credit card meant for a beginner. If you already have a checking or savings account, check to see if your bank has a credit card for someone with limited credit history. If you can't get a credit card at your current bank, there are still more options.

These are some of the most famous credit cards that most people want to have in their wallet.

In order to get one, there is a **major secret** that they don't tell you.

Get a **Savings and Checking account** and make sure you have at least a **$2,000 minimum of cash** in the bank. The real secret is that if you have a substantial amount of cash in your Savings or checking account, chances are you will be approved despite credit history.

Once you have money in your account, they see that you can cover any credit card bill. So start out with a lower credit card limit of about $250.00 dollars. Purchase a small item and pay it off quickly. If you do this **3 times**, they will *<u>raise your credit limit</u>*. They will take into account that you can *<u>pay off debts quickly</u>*. Even if you have the cash for it, **small purchases only**, then when the bill comes in, **pay it off immediately.**

The problem with credit is that we tend to make large purchases we cannot pay off quickly. This results in credit card default and unable to pay credit card balances.

Credit is not a given and has to be earned. If you earn it the right way, this could boost your credit score when you wish to purchase a larger ticket items such as a Car or House in the future.

Big loans such as a business or refinance to a larger investment will be in your favor when credit scores are involved.

Get the credit you deserve by paying off the balance quickly on small purchases. You will see the financial freedom of credit and your scores.

Chapter 6 – Get a Second Income

Taken from the website:

http://www.quickanddirtytips.com/money-finance/saving-spending/how-find-second-source-income?page=all

By **Laura Adams, MBA'; Money Girl**

See more at: http://www.quickanddirtytips.com/money-finance/saving-spending/how-find-second-source-income?page=all#sthash.0irkTJ4C.dpuf

Almost everyone wants to make more money, but when you feel like you can barely keep up with your full-time job, the idea of taking on a second or even third one can sound a little ridiculous. After all, if you're already squeezed for time, then how can you possibly pick up even more responsibilities?

How to Find a Second Source of Income

As daunting as it sounds, finding multiple sources of income doesn't have to be difficult, and it can be the solution to achieving more financial stability. In this article I'll give you solid tips for how to create extra sources of income that can pick up slack in your budget, make it easier to save money, and give you an automatic safety net in case you unexpectedly lose your job.

Why You Need Multiple Sources of Income

I like to think about having an additional source of income as being sort of like an insurance policy. I interviewed one young woman who taught aerobics classes in the evenings after spending her days working as a videographer for news organizations. When she was unexpectedly laid off from her day job, she quickly doubled her aerobics teaching load and was able to keep herself afloat until she found a new full-time job. Some more examples of income multi-streaming are a teacher I know who sells used baby clothes out of her home and a young couple who run a small Internet business on the weekends. Just like these people, you can also pick a profitable project or create a business that matches your lifestyle.

How to Start Making More Money

Making more money, or multi-streaming your income doesn't have to be quite as overwhelming as it first sounds. If you're ready to get started, here are six ways to begin picking up an extra paycheck:

Extra Income Tip #1: Share Your Skills

The first step is to think about what you can do that's unusual or valuable to other people. Do you know a second language well enough to teach it to others, or have a skill like woodworking, crochet, or playing a musical instrument? People pay for all kinds of lessons. Just log onto the "services" section at Craigslist.org to start brainstorming what you could offer. If you're not sure whether there's a market for your skill, post an ad on Craigslist or on a local message board and see whether anyone contacts you about it.

Extra Income Tip #2: Start a Service Business

The first step is to think about what you can do that's unusual or valuable to other people.

People are willing to pay for all kinds of things, like house-sitting, dog-walking, cooking, yard work, cleaning, exterior pressure washing, computer work, tutoring, and even organization. If you're interested in [launching a business](#), come up with a business plan and start spreading the word.

Extra Income Tip #3: Sell Your Creativity

There are websites like [Cafepress.com](#) that let users design their own T-shirts and products with witty words or fun graphics and then sell them for a profit. Though you won't get rich if just friends and family members bite, you could turn into a success story if you create a design at just the right time.

For example, if a big news event or viral video inspires you, then quickly make a related T-shirt and get the word out. After President Obama signed the health care bill into law last year, Vice President Biden uttered a memorable expletive, and almost immediately T-shirts emblazoned with "Health insurance reform is a big #@%*! Deal" became hot sellers!

Extra Income Tip #4: Get Crafty

Websites like [Etsy.com](#) make it easy to start selling your own jewelry, artwork, and other handiwork. But don't get stuck making 100 beaded necklaces for $2 each. For the biggest payoff, stick with projects that have a relatively low time-to-profit ratio.

Extra Income Tip #5: Market Your Knowledge

The creator of [MochaManual.com](#), The Black Mom's Guide to Life, became a consultant to companies that wanted to better understand the concerns and preferences of African American mothers. You can also become a paid consultant or speaker once you've developed your reputation as an expert. A local speaker's association can help you find gigs and negotiate a rate for making presentations. You might even consider checking to see whether the local community college is interested in having you teach a course in your subject area.

Extra Income Tip #6: Sell an Unusual Service

The website Fiverr.com lets people sell (and buy) all kinds of wacky services for just $5 a pop. Current services for sale include designing a visually-appealing signature, creating a customized sound effect, making a tough decision, and writing a personalized rap song. Just as with crafty projects, you don't want to over commit to something that won't earn you a big return, but if you have a skill that easily translates into a quick service, then this could be a good strategy for you.

These are just a few ideas to get you thinking about what you can do to create a multi-streamed income. Your project might turn into a full-time job in itself or it could just be a back-up plan that gives you peace of mind while you continue to work a day job. Finding extra work that you really enjoy can be a great way to share your skills, meet new people, and take your personal finances to the next level.

This article was written by Kimberly Palmer, the author of *Generation Earn: The Young Professional's Guide to Spending, Investing, and Giving Back*, who writes the Alpha Consumer blog at usnews.com/alpha. It was edited and read in the podcast by Laura Adams.

- See more at: http://www.quickanddirtytips.com/money-finance/saving-spending/how-find-second-source-income?page=all#sthash.lQAcHXWf.dpuf

Bottom Line: A second source of income is good to help you pay those additional bills that your primary income cannot.

Plus, look at how additional monies can help pay for the things you need to purchase as well as allow you to be financially free of money.

Chapter 7: Invest in the Future

Taken from the website:

http://www.ey.com/US/en/Industries/Financial-Services/Asset-Management/2011-wealth-management-study---investing-in-the-future---Wealth-management-product-demand

Nearly all firms have invested or expect to invest in technology to support their wealth management advisors. This is important because these advisors work in the important areas of asset gathering, servicing and investment selection.

Identifying investment opportunities

Wealth management firms are investing across a broad spectrum of technologies, headcount and processes not only to support their product and client strategies, but also to meet new regulatory requirements.

80% of firms have invested in technology to support client reporting.

Wealth management firms with over 100k clients report a broad range of areas they have or expect to invest in, including:
- Back office execution
- Client on-boarding
- Client reporting

In which of the following areas have you invested in the past year? In which of the following areas do you expect to invest in the next year?

Technology

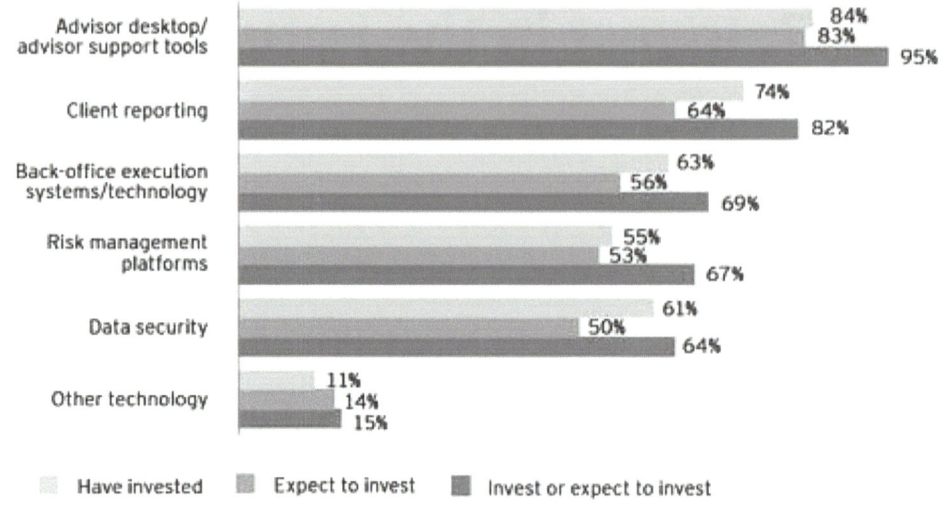

People and processes

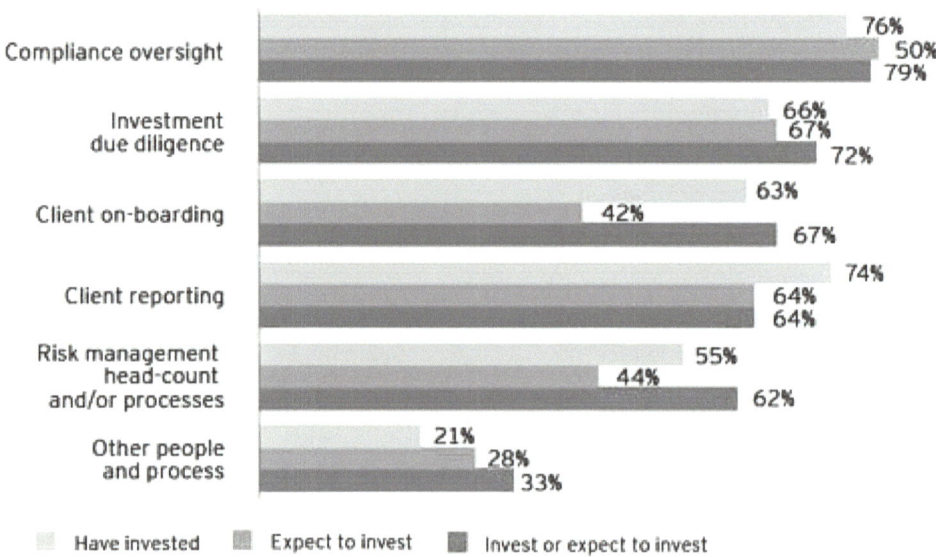

Source: Greenwich Associates
Note: Chart based on 39 respondents. Percentages do not total to 100% due to multiple responses by survey respondents.

Primary drivers for investment

Our survey found firms targeting largely mass-market clients were somewhat less likely to say they were targeting revenue growth and much more focused on efficiencies and improving client experience.

Those targeting high-net-worth clients were more likely to attribute investments in the due diligence process to growing top-line revenue than those firms targeting primarily mass-market clients — most likely because of the broader range of alternative investments offered to clients and the robustness of the due diligence process that is required.

What were the primary drivers for the investments you just described? Please tell me the primary reason(s) you invested or expect to invest, individually. [Advisor desktop/advisor support tools]

Areas of investment (expected and current)	Regulatory compliance	Revenue growth	Cost or operational efficiencies	Improved client experience
Advisor desktop/advisor support tools (38)	34%	71%	84%	71%
Back-office execution systems/technology (30)	37%	30%	90%	60%
Risk management platforms (27)	74%	22%	59%	41%
Client reporting (32)	31%	38%	56%	91%
Data security (26)	65%	8%	73%	35%
Client on-boarding (26)	42%	54%	77%	77%
Investment due diligence (27)	67%	41%	56%	52%
Compliance oversight (29)	86%	7%	55%	34%

Source: Greenwich Associates
Note: Number in parentheses represents the number of respondents.

Changes to mitigate company risk

The majority of firms we interviewed have taken multiple steps to mitigate risk through investments in:
- Client investment suitability
- Manager selection due diligence
- Monitoring (performance and risk)

In which area do you expect to invest the most?

Overall

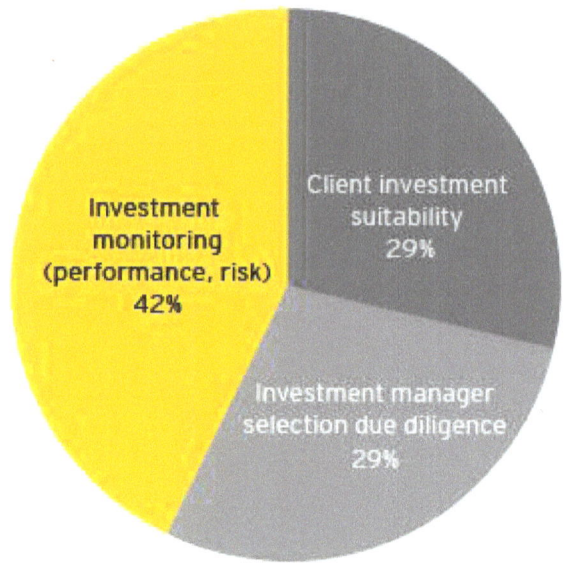

Segment	Base	Investment monitoring	Investment manager due diligence	Client investment suitability
HNW*	(20)	40%	45%	15%
MM*	(15)	47%	7%	47%

*HNW – high-net-worth; MM – mass market

Source: Greenwich Associates
Note: Chart based on 35 respondents.

Alternative investments

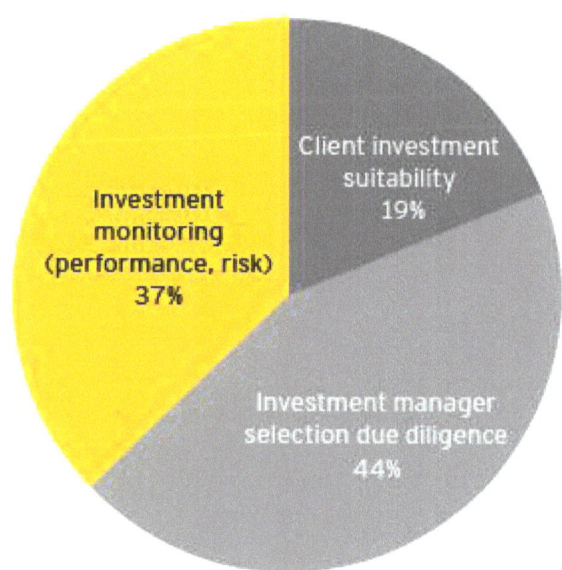

Segment	Base	Investment monitoring	Investment manager due diligence	Client investment suitability
HNW*	(17)	29%	53%	20%
MM*	(10)	50%	30%	43%

*HNW – high-net-worth; MM – mass market

Source: Greenwich Associates
Note: Chart based on 27 respondents.

Transparency in manager due diligence process

Overall, fewer than half of the wealth managers we interviewed said they had increased transparency into the investment manager selection process over the past year.

The largest firms — those with more than $150b in assets under management — were least likely to have offered additional transparency into the process, with more than 80% saying they have not made any changes.

Those that do offer more transparency said they improved client marketing materials and have been educating clients through direct conversations about the due diligence process.

In the past year, have you increased transparency to clients in the investment manager selection process?

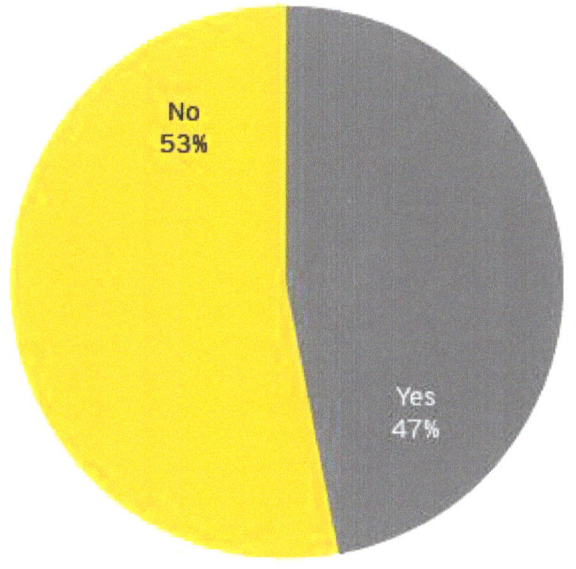

Source: Greenwich Associates
Note: Chart based on 38 respondents.

Plans for adapting to the new fiduciary standard

Wealth managers have been proactive in multiple areas as they adapt to the new fiduciary standard. They have been investing in additional advisor training and enhancing disclosures and processes for client suitability.

Interestingly, far fewer said that they were rationalizing their product offerings and limiting their product range.

Those targeting the mass market are much more apt (73% versus 55% for those targeting high-net-worth clients) to revisit their suitability processes, but little difference in expectations was evident elsewhere.

How is your firm planning to adapt to the new "fiduciary standard"?

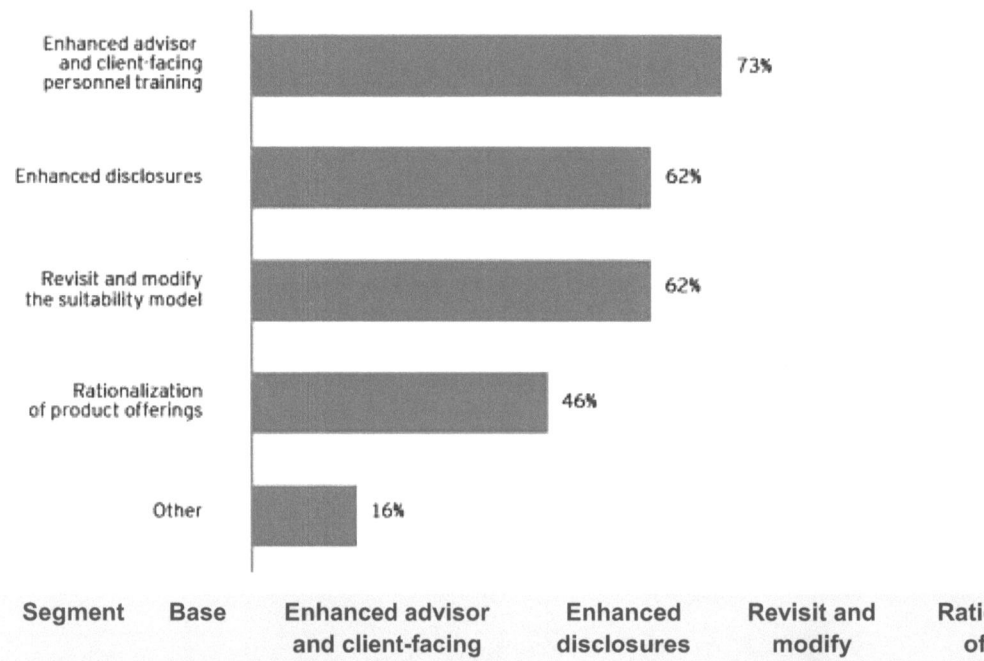

Segment	Base	Enhanced advisor and client-facing personnel training	Enhanced disclosures	Revisit and modify suitability model	Rationalization of product offerings	Other
HNW*	(22)	73%	64%	55%	45%	14%
MM*	(15)	73%	60%	73%	47%	20%

HNW – high-net-worth; MM – mass market

Source: Greenwich Associates
Note: Chart based on 37 respondents. Percentages do not total to 100% due to multiple responses by survey respondents.

It is important for firms to have a benchmark for which products firms are actively selling and their growth expectations as they expand their offerings.

What products do you sell?

Nearly all of the wealth management firms we interviewed offer mutual funds and three in four offer ETFs. The disparity between ETFs and mutual funds sold, especially in light of the lower fee structure, may be a reflection of the maturity of the two markets.

Additionally, nearly all wealth management firms offer managed accounts, but just half offer unified managed accounts. For those firms that actively sell managed accounts, nearly 40% of the wealth management firms expect annual growth in AUMs to exceed 15%.

 In each of the following individual product categories, please describe Whether you actively sell the product?

Product demand — managed accounts

Overall, separately managed and mutual fund wrap accounts are the two most actively sold managed accounts.

Investment professionals targeting high-net-worth clients are significantly more optimistic about AUM growth in unified managed accounts, advisor-directed managed accounts and ETF wrap accounts. Those wealth management firms targeting the mass-market clients are much more optimistic about growth of mutual fund wrap accounts.

 In each of the following individual product categories, please describe Whether you actively sell the product?

Product demand — unified managed household accounts

Only 28% of the wealth management firms interviewed offer unified managed household accounts (UMHAs) and there were no major distinctions across the various segment types. Wealth management firms of larger scale were slightly more prone to offer UMHAs than their smaller counterparts.

Because of the relative newness of this product, we did note varying definitions of the UMHAs and a lack of consistency with respect to product features.

Firms not currently offering this product may need to evaluate their competitive positions.

Does your firm have an annual product review?

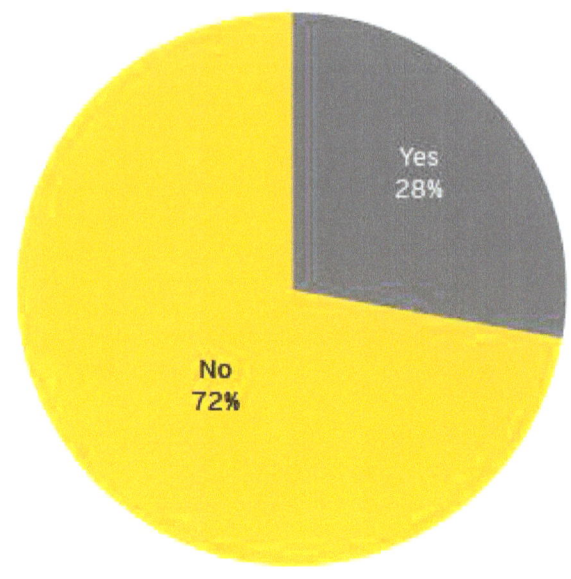

Source: Greenwich Associates
Note: Chart based on 36 respondents.

Which one or two aspects of UMHAs are most challenging?

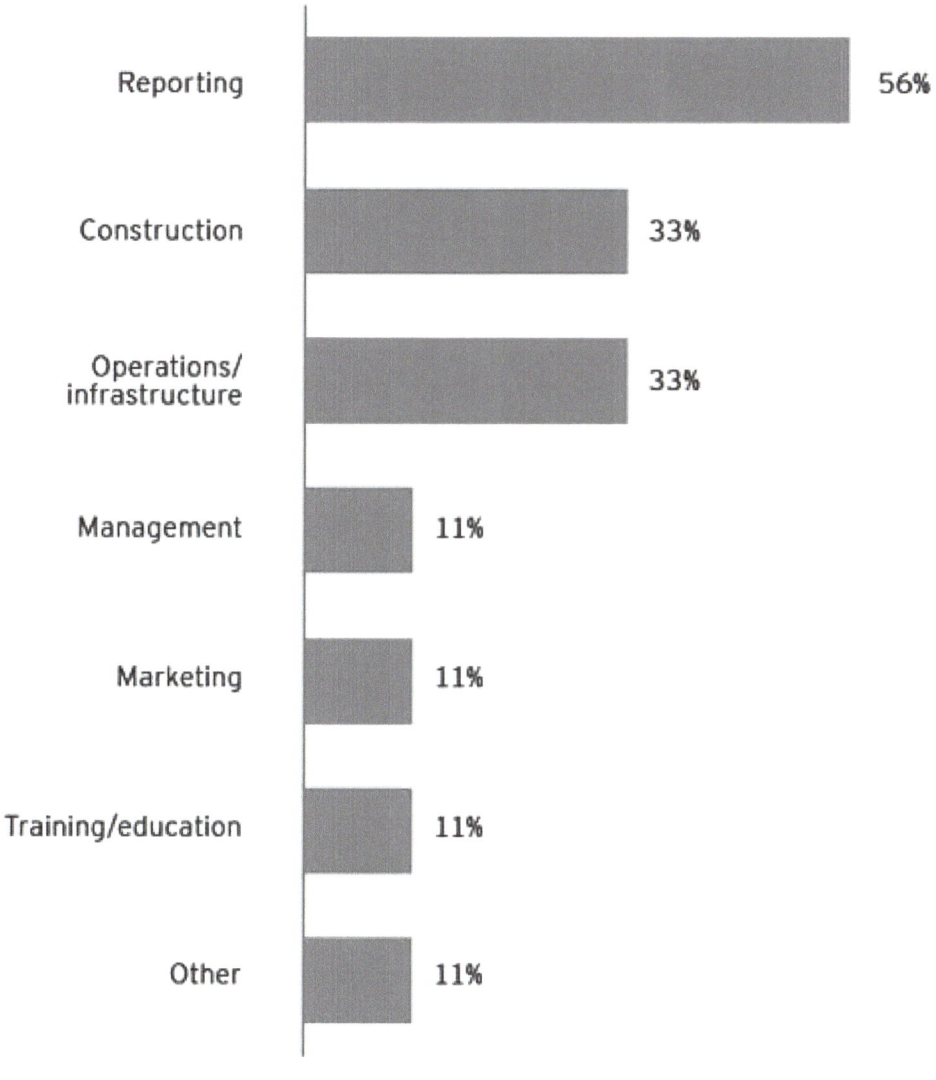

Local.com/Retirement__Investments

Source: Greenwich Associates
Note: Chart based on 9 respondents. Percentages do not total to 100% due to multiple responses by survey respondents.

Best-performing asset classes

Product strategy and product management professionals at leading wealth management firms expect emerging market equities and US equities to be the best-performing asset classes over the next two years, and the outlook is fairly consistent across small and large firms.

Based on your capital market assumptions, what do you expect will be the best-performing asset classes over the next two years?

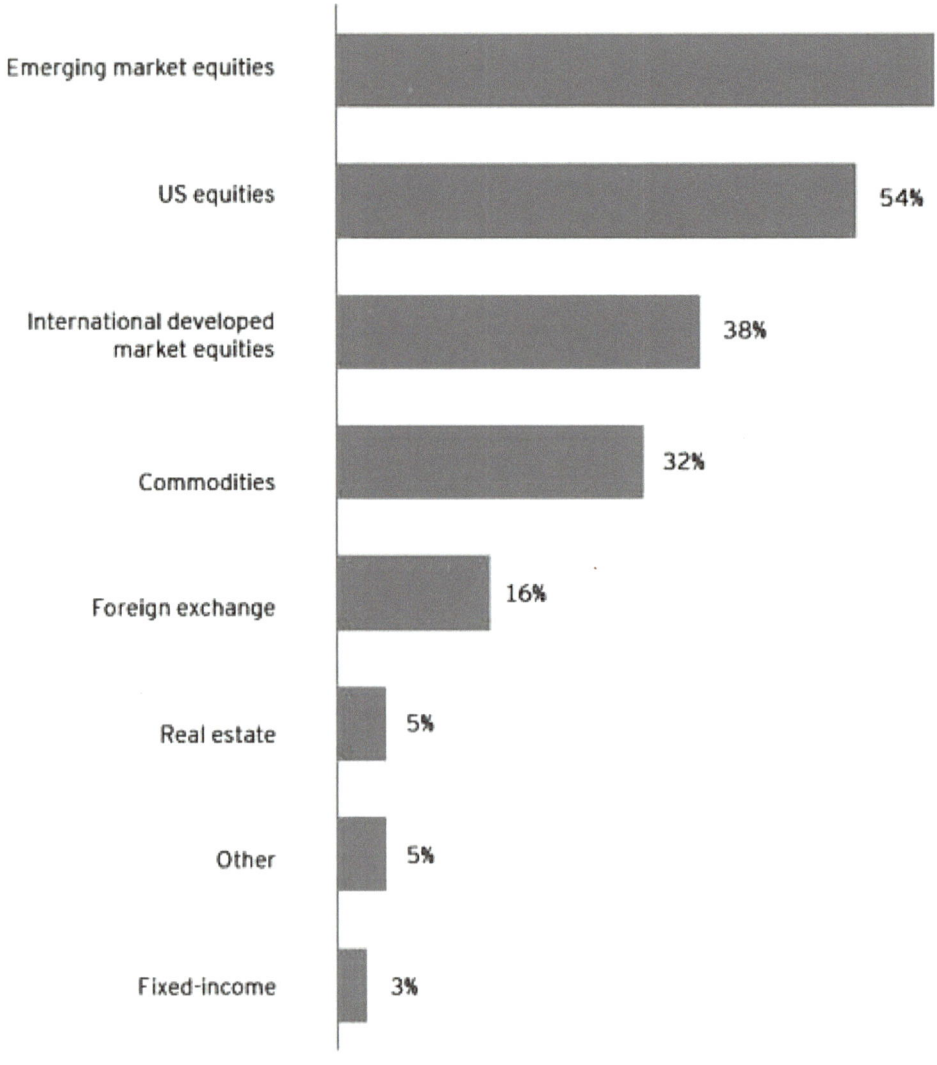

Local.com/Retirement__Investments

Source: Greenwich Associates
Note: Chart based on 9 respondents. Percentages do not total to 100% due to multiple responses by survey respondents.

This was a study done in 2011 about technology firms investing for the future. It is important to learn how businesses invest in the future, so you can understand how you can invest in the future for yourself.

Ernest & Young an Accountant firm, did a study on wealth management product demand and how firms invest in the future.

Overall, the summary shows that if companies invest in the future, so should you.

Investing in the future is as easy as understanding the trends in the market. Read **Financial Freedom One: A Special Guide to Understanding Investing.** **Read pages 42 to 46, 51** on Trends in the market and how to read them.

Research and learn about future trends in the stock and bond markets. Read on market timing and analyst.

Please do your homework before you invest in real estate, investments commodities, stocks, bonds etc.

Speak to professionals and get consultation from financial advisors before making any decisions.

Your future depends on how much research you do and understand where the trends in the market are located. Watch the news and look for opportunities in the market and chart your course to Financial Freedom.

Taken from the website:

http://budgeting.thenest.com/invest-money-future-3713.html
How to Invest Your Money for the Future
By Bonnie Conrad, Demand Media

Invest your money wisely

No matter what you do for a living or how much or how little money you make, investing for the future is critical. These days, fewer workers than ever can rely on a traditional defined benefit pension plan, so it is up to every worker to save for his own retirement. Learning to save and invest for the future is very important, and that process should start as soon as you start earning your own money.

Sponsored Link
7% Annual Annuity Return
Get guaranteed lifetime income and reduced risks to retirees all here.
AdvisorWorld.com/Compare Annuities

Step 1

Build an emergency fund equal to at least three to six months' worth of living expenses. Having an emergency fund in place will protect you in the event of a job loss, large medical expense or other financial shock.

Step 2

Check with your employer and ask if there is a 401k plan in place. Request an enrollment booklet and review it carefully. Invest at least enough to get the full company match, but aim to invest more than that over time. Consider enrolling in an automatic escalation plan that boosts your contribution percentage automatically each year you remain in the plan. As of 2010, you can invest up to $16,500 in a 401k plan, plus another $5,500 if you are 50 or older. The administrator of the plan will keep track of your contributions and suspend them once you reach the limit for the year.

Step 3

Contact several mutual fund companies to ask about their individual retirement account, or IRA, plans. The IRA is designed to help workers save for retirement by providing a tax break, either up front in the case of a traditional IRA or through tax-free withdrawals in the case of a Roth. In addition to mutual fund companies, banks and brokerage firms can administer your IRA for you as well. As of 2010, the contribution limit for IRA accounts is $5,000, plus an extra $1,000 for those age 50 and older.

Step 4

Set up an automatic monthly investment into your IRA by directing money to be transferred from your bank account to the mutual fund within the IRA. This automatic investment forces you to save and also forces you to live on less than you earn.

Step 5

Set up similar automatic investments for mutual funds outside your IRA and 401k if you still have money to invest. Investing a set amount of money each month means you automatically buy more shares when the market is down and fewer when it is at all-time highs. This approach, known as dollar cost averaging, is an excellent way to build wealth for the long term

In building your wealth, invest your money for the future according to your needs. If you are looking to plan for retirement or plan to purchase a house, car or business. Make the investment as earlier as possible by setting goals, savings and looking at the progress towards your goal.

Hopefully this book will help you chart your course in life and allow you to build, plan & Invest in the future.

www.ingramcontent.com/pod-product-compliance
Lightning Source LLC
Chambersburg PA
CBHW050801180526
45159CB00004B/1512